Author:

Fiona Macdonald studied history at
Cambridge University, England, and at the
University of East Anglia. She has taught in
schools, adult education, and universities, and
is the author of numerous books for children.

Series creator:

David Salariya was born in Dundee,
Scotland. He has illustrated a wide range of books
and has created and designed many new series
for publishers in the UK and overseas. David
established The Salariya Book Company in 1989.
He lives in Brighton, England, with his wife,
illustrator Shirley Willis, and their son, Jonathan.

Artists:

Bryan Beach
David Pavon
Caroline Romanet
Andy Rowland
Paco Sordo
Diego Vaisberg

Editor:

Jacqueline Ford

© The Salariya Book Company Ltd MMXVIII

No part of this publication may be reproduced in whole or in
part, or stored in a retrieval system, or transmitted in any form or
by any means, electronic, mechanical, photocopying, recording,
or otherwise, without written permission of the publisher. For
information regarding permission, write to the copyright holder.

Published in Great Britain in 2018 by
The Salariya Book Company Ltd
25 Marlborough Place, Brighton BN1 1UB

ISBN-13: 978-0-531-23144-9 (lib. bdg.) 978-0-531-23239-2 (pbk.)

All rights reserved.
Published in 2018 in the United States
by Franklin Watts
An imprint of Scholastic Inc.

A CIP catalog record for this book is available
from the Library of Congress.

Printed and bound in China.
Printed on paper from sustainable sources.
1 2 3 4 5 6 7 8 9 10 R 27 26 25 24 23 22 21 20 19 18

SCHOLASTIC, FRANKLIN WATTS, and associated logos are
trademarks and/or registered trademarks of Scholastic Inc.

PAPER FROM
SUSTAINABLE
FORESTS

The Science of Snot and Phlegm

The Slimy Truth About Breathing

Written by
Fiona Macdonald

Franklin Watts®
An Imprint of Scholastic Inc.

Contents

Introduction

Breathe in, breathe out—we all do it, every day and every night. Breathing is essential for life. It brings oxygen (a gas in the air) into our lungs. We need oxygen to keep our brains and bodies working properly. Without it—without breathing—we would die very quickly!

Usually we don't notice that we are breathing; it happens automatically. But sometimes, when we have a cold, or asthma or hay fever, we find breathing difficult. Our noses, throats, windpipes, and lungs become clogged with sticky, slippery mucus; that's the scientific name for snot and phlegm. We sniff and snort and cough and blow our noses.

Too much snot and phlegm can look gross and make us feel miserable, but normally, they're very useful. Read on, and find out more....

The Breath Of Life

Oxygen In...

Inside the lungs, oxygen passes through the thin walls of millions of alveoli (air sacs) into capillaries (tiny tubes) carrying blood. Then red blood cells carry the oxygen through our body, where it reacts with nutrients from our food to release the energy we need.

Blood to heart

Blood from heart

Alveoli

Capillaries

On average, we use over 145 gallons (550 liters) of oxygen every day. An amazing 20 percent is taken by the brain. It needs lots of energy to fuel the electrical signals it uses to function.

The body parts used for breathing are known as our respiratory system. Together, they keep us alive. Each part has a special function. When we breathe in, air containing oxygen is sucked through our nose and throat, down our windpipe, and into our lungs. When we breathe out, our lungs puff waste gases (carbon dioxide and water vapor) back up again and out into the air. From our nose right through to our lungs, our respiratory system is coated with sticky, slippery mucus. This works like oil in a machine to keep the system running smoothly. We need mucus to breathe!

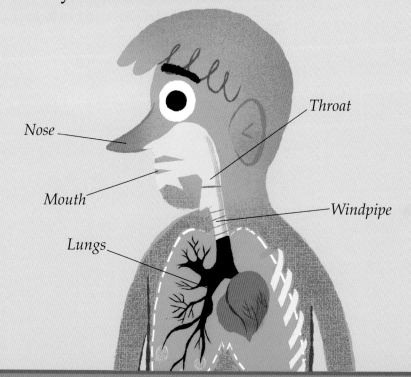

Nose

Throat

Mouth

Windpipe

Lungs

...Waste Gases Out

While oxygen passes through the alveoli in one direction, waste gases travel the opposite way, from red blood cells into the lungs. Waste gases are produced when our bodies use energy. They are toxic, so we get rid of them by breathing out.

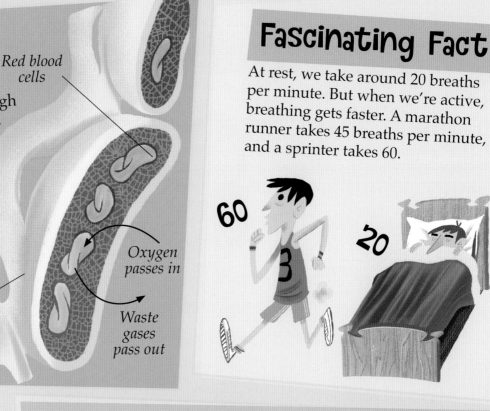

Red blood cells

Oxygen passes in

Waste gases pass out

Alveoli

Fascinating Fact

At rest, we take around 20 breaths per minute. But when we're active, breathing gets faster. A marathon runner takes 45 breaths per minute, and a sprinter takes 60.

The air we breathe contains:
78.09% Nitrogen
20.95% Oxygen
0.93% Argon
0.039% Carbon dioxide
plus tiny amounts of rare gases. It may also contain up to 1% water vapor.

Mighty Muscles

The power to move air through our respiratory system comes from muscles in our chest, back, and abdomen. When we breathe in, a muscle called the diaphragm sinks down, creating low pressure inside the chest. That makes air flow in. When we breathe out, the diaphragm pushes upward, squeezing air from our lungs.

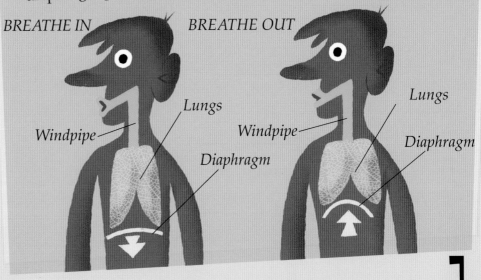

BREATHE IN

BREATHE OUT

Windpipe

Lungs

Diaphragm

Windpipe

Lungs

Diaphragm

Protect and Survive

Don't pick your nose! It's better and safer to blow. Snot is often full of viruses and bacteria; you don't want to get them on your fingers or spread them around.

What Does Snot Say About You?

Normal snot is clear and runny. But when you're sick, it can change color.

White: inflamed nose lining

Yellow: you have a cold

Green: bacterial infection

Red: your nose is bleeding

Brown: there's dirt up your nose

Black: a fungus—see a doctor!

Snot and phlegm act as powerful defenders, guarding the places where germs, dirt, dust, and other dangerous, irritating substances might enter the body. Mucus surrounds and captures all these "invaders," forming extra-thick, sticky snot and phlegm that can be removed by coughing or blowing our nose. Mucus also carries white cells from our blood that fight harmful bacteria. And it protects the delicate inner surfaces of our respiratory system by stopping them from becoming rough, dry, scratched, or cracked.

Oh no, I don't think snot is meant to be that color!

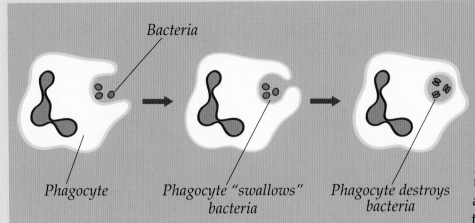

Bacteria

Phagocyte

Phagocyte "swallows" bacteria

Phagocyte destroys bacteria

Germ Eaters

Mucus in the respiratory system contains millions of phagocytes: special white blood cells that "eat" and destroy disease-causing bacteria. Fresh phagocytes are produced by the body all the time. Old, dead phagocytes are carried out of our nose or throat in phlegm and snot.

How Much?!

On average, we produce between 3.5 and 5 cups (1 and 1.5 L) of mucus every day, mostly in our nose and lungs. But mucus is also produced in other body parts, such as our stomach and intestines. It shields their delicate linings, and helps food and waste matter move smoothly along.

I hope I don't drop this!

Mucus contains lysozyme, an enzyme (natural chemical catalyst) that fights infection. This was discovered when snot dripped from scientist Alexander Fleming's nose into a dish of bacteria—and killed them!

Disgusting Data

Healthy mucus is stretchy because it contains mucins, which are chemicals produced in several different parts of our body. Mucins are shaped like long, microscopic threads. They tangle and stick to each other—just like cooked spaghetti—forming slimy, slippery, stretchy snot.

Why Do Noses Run?

Our noses keep growing until we are about 19 years old. Then they stop. But as we get older, they droop and sag and look longer.

W hen we're healthy, special cells in the lining of the nose produce just enough mucus to keep it working properly. The main function of our nose is to warm the air as it enters our body. This helps keep our body temperature steady. At the same time, mucus in the nose—and hair in our nostrils—traps dust and dirt. But if our nose lining is inflamed or infected, mucus cells produce extra snot, and that drips out. It has to go somewhere!

Drip, Drip, It's Freezing!

There's another reason for runny noses: cold weather! When icy air enters our nostrils, capillaries inside the nose fill with lots of warm blood to try to heat the air. But the extra blood also encourages mucus cells to produce more snot.

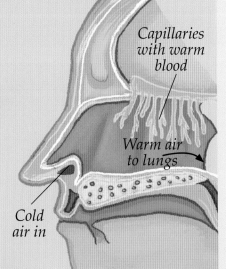

Capillaries with warm blood

Warm air to lungs

Cold air in

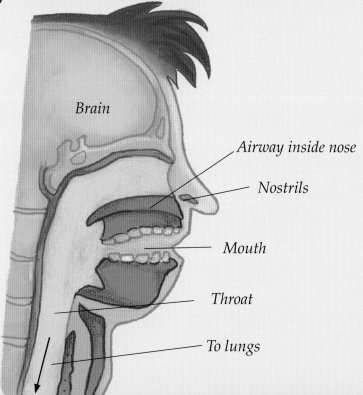

Brain

Airway inside nose

Nostrils

Mouth

Throat

To lungs

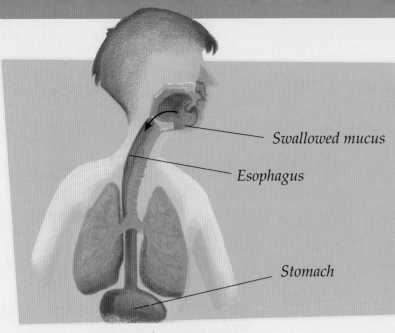

Swallowed mucus

Esophagus

Stomach

Sniff and Swallow

We cough, spit, and blow our noses to get rid of snot and phlegm, but most of the mucus we produce each day ends up in our stomach. We swallow it without noticing. Strong acids in the stomach kill any viruses or bacteria in the mucus. Then it's digested along with the rest of our food.

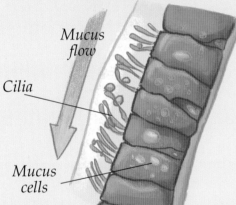

Mucus flow

Cilia

Mucus cells

Keep It Moving

Cilia (microscopic "fingers") grow in the lining of our respiratory system. They bend very gently from side to side to push mucus along. This ensures that normal quantities of snot and phlegm do not cause blockages, all the way from our nose to our lungs.

Noses grow in all sorts of different shapes and sizes. The longest human nose recorded so far measures 3.46 inches (8.8 centimeters). It belongs to a man named Mehmet Ozyurek of Turkey.

Disgusting Data

The average person grows a total of 6.5 feet (2 meters) of nostril hair in a lifetime. Usually, the hairs fall out when they're about 0.39 of an inch (1 cm) long. But in some people, especially older men, they stay in place and keep on growing.

What mustache?

11

Sinuses, Tonsils, and Adenoids

Got sinusitis? Sip plenty of water or warm drinks. They will help make mucus thinner, so it drains away more easily.

Ouch! Trapped Mucus...

Sometimes, mucus can become a breeding ground for disease-causing bacteria. Or, sinuses can get filled by trapped snot and mucus. In either case, pressure is put on the surrounding skin and bone, causing pain and inflammation. This is called sinusitis.

What are sinuses, tonsils, and adenoids? Sinuses are hollow spaces within our skull bones, above and below our eyes. Tonsils and adenoids grow in our throat and at the back of our nose. They are made of millions of red and white blood cells inside spongy lymph tissue. Sinuses, tonsils, and adenoids all help our breathing. Sinuses warm the air that flows into our bodies. Tonsils and adenoids trap cells that might cause disease, keeping us healthy and breathing easily.

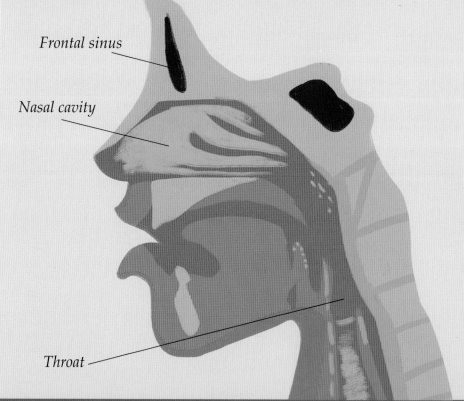

Frontal sinus

Nasal cavity

Throat

  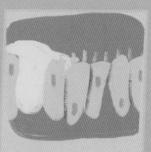

Normal, healthy cilia

Sinusitis: lining inflamed; cilia cannot move

Repeated sinusitis: lining scarred; cilia destroyed

Sinus Scars

In sinusitis, bacteria attack the lining of sinuses and the nose, and white blood cells rush to fight them. The resulting inflammation can sometimes leave scars. These damage cilia, so they can no longer move mucus away. Our sinuses become even more blocked with snot.

Enlarged adenoids

Enlarged tonsils

Throat

Windpipe

Infected Defenders

For most of the time, tonsils and adenoids help fight disease. But if they become infected, they can swell and narrow the airways in our nose and throat. This is painful and makes breathing very difficult. It can also make our breath smell horrible!

Tonsils are made of tough, spongy tissue. They are so rubbery that if you threw them on the floor they would bounce like a ball!

Fascinating Fact

Tra-la-la! Large, clear healthy sinus spaces in the bones of the skull make the voice sound clearer, more resonant (ringing), and musical. They also work like echo chambers, making the voice louder. A lot of opera singers have lovely sinuses!

13

The Cold Virus

Handkerchiefs were invented in China over 2,000 years ago, but were too expensive for ordinary people. Instead, they wiped their noses on rags, leaves, dried grass—or on their sleeves!

The Life Cycle of a Cold

We all catch colds, sometimes several times a year. They are the most common human infection—up to a billion occur each winter in the United States. In the past, people thought that getting wet or chilled caused a cold—the clue was in the name! But today we know that colds are caused by viruses, tiny organisms that invade the cells of living creatures. We are most likely to catch a cold when we are tired or stressed, or when our nose and throat are already irritated, for example by dust or pollution.

DAYS 2–3. Now you're sniffling and sneezing. You may feel tired, shivery, and achy. Your nose and throat are sore. Rest, drink lots of water, and get those tissues ready!

DAYS 1–2. You've caught a cold! You still feel okay, but the virus is growing inside you, attacking the lining of your respiratory system.

DAYS 3–5. Snot central! Your nose runs and runs. At first the mucus is clear, but it may change to white, yellow, or green as white blood cells hurry to your nose and throat to fight against the cold virus. Perhaps spend a day in bed.

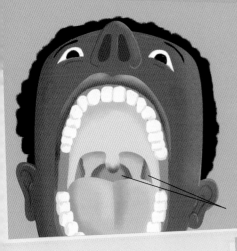

Virus...

The virus that causes colds can inflame our throats as well. Your throat may look pink and feel sore and scratchy, but the pain does not last for long.

Red swollen throat and tonsils

Ahhhhh...

...Or Bacteria?

When bacteria attack our throat, the pain is worse and longer-lasting. Our throat may look dark red, our tongue may be gray and furry, and our tonsils may be swollen and dotted with white ulcers.

White spots

Gray furry tongue

DAYS 5–6. Cough it up! Some mucus runs down to your lungs. The lungs also produce phlegm (mucus mixed with white blood cells and watery secretions). You cough and spit to get rid of it. Rest if you're feeling sick or have a headache or raised temperature.

DAYS 7–10. Feeling better? Most people do by this time. Your body has fought off the cold virus. Good job!

Fascinating Fact

There are over 300 different viruses that can cause a cold in humans. They mutate (change) all the time. That's why colds are so common and why it is so difficult to find a cure.

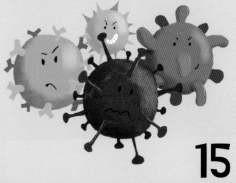

Bright sunlight makes some people sneeze. No one really knows why. It's a medical mystery!

Allergic Reactions

An allergen is a substance that irritates or inflames. When it contacts body parts, white blood cells release a chemical called histamine. The histamine binds (joins) to nerve cells, causing an allergic reaction—sneezing, itching, and lots of mucus. Antihistamine medicines stop this from happening.

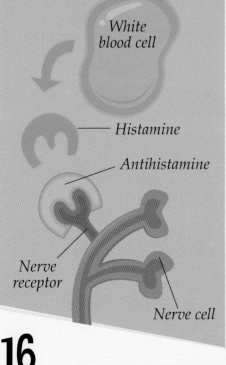

White blood cell

—— *Histamine*

—— *Antihistamine*

Nerve receptor

Nerve cell

What Is Hay Fever?

In the past, people made hay to feed cattle in winter. They had no machines to help them; they cut and dried the grass by hand. Although the hay makers didn't have colds or flu, they sneezed and sniffled while they worked. Their noses dripped with mucus or were blocked with snot; their throats were sore; their eyes were itchy and full of tears. They had "hay fever." The lining of their eyes and their respiratory system was inflamed by microscopic grains of pollen, produced by grass and many other plants.

Why Do We Sneeze?

When the inside of our nose gets irritated, nerves send signals to a "sneeze center" in our brain. This sends messages to muscles in different parts of our body, telling them to squeeze tight and push the irritating substance out of our nose.

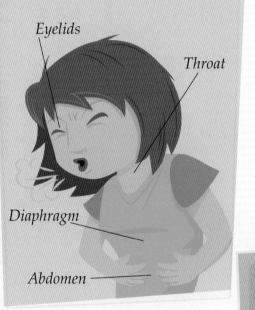

Eyelids

Throat

Diaphragm

Abdomen

It's very hard to keep our eyes open when we sneeze. Sneezing is a reflex (automatic) action. All the muscles involved are activated by a part of our brain that we can't control.

What Else Triggers Allergies?

Plant pollen is a powerful allergen; it still causes hay fever today. Other common allergens include spicy foods, household chemicals, pet hair and dander (flakes of skin), and tiny mites (spiderlike creatures) that live in the dust in our homes.

Disgusting Data

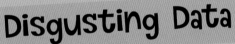

Have you heard the old saying, "Coughs and sneezes spread diseases"? Here's how and why. When you sneeze, tiny drops of snot and saliva fly out of your nose and mouth at up to 49 miles (79 kilometers) per hour, scattering viruses and bacteria all around. This is why you should always try to cover your mouth when you sneeze.

It's a vicious circle! The more mucus we produce, the more inflamed the lining of our respiratory system becomes. So we produce even more mucus!

Steam

A good way to clear a stuffy, snotty nose is by breathing warm, wet steam in a bath or a shower. The water vapor softens thick, sticky mucus, helping it to drain away.

Too Much!

Mucus is important, but sometimes we can have too much of it. Colds, flu, and allergic reactions can all leave our respiratory system full of sticky, slimy mucus, and our trash cans stacked with soggy tissues. Producing so much mucus inflames the lining of our nose and throat. So this swells, causing pain and pressure, and leaving less space for air to flow down into our lungs. As a result, we find it very hard to breathe!

I can't take much more of this!

Smells Nice, but Does It Work?

In the past, people thought that strong-smelling mixtures of herbs and spices, rubbed on the chest—or the feet!—could help clear snot and phlegm. The warmth of the body made vapors from the mixtures rise up into the nose. These may have soothed irritated airways and made the patient feel better, but strong smells were not a cure for anything!

Decongestants

Medicines called decongestants shrink swollen capillaries in the lining of the nose. This widens the airway, eases breathing, and helps clear mucus blockages.

Unfortunately, some decongestant medicines can also give patients a headache or make them feel sick.

One surprising—and simple—way to help clear catarrh (extra-thick, sticky mucus) is to wash out the nose with salt water—a natural disinfectant.

Fascinating Fact

People with broken noses often suffer badly from catarrh and sinus infections. Why? Because the lining of their nose is torn or damaged by scars, so cilia can't sweep mucus away, or because the airway inside is narrowed or twisted. So snot gets blocked—and bacteria grow.

Why Do We Cough?

We can't control most coughs. They are reflex (automatic) actions, and happen whether we want them to or not. There's a famous saying that "Love and a cough can't be hid."

Why Do Coughs Keep Us Awake?

We cough more at night because when we lie down in bed, mucus from our nose, throat, and sinuses runs down into our lungs. We cough to try to bring it back up again.

A hem! Wheeze! Cough, cough! Feel a tickle in your throat or a crackle in your chest? Your body is trying to protect you! When we cough, our diaphragm muscles push air out of our lungs at high speed. With luck, unwanted substances are forced out as well. The most usual reason for coughing is a cold or the flu. Then, we cough to get rid of snot and phlegm. But anything that irritates our lungs can cause us to cough, from exhaust fumes, mold, and perfume to spicy cooking smells.

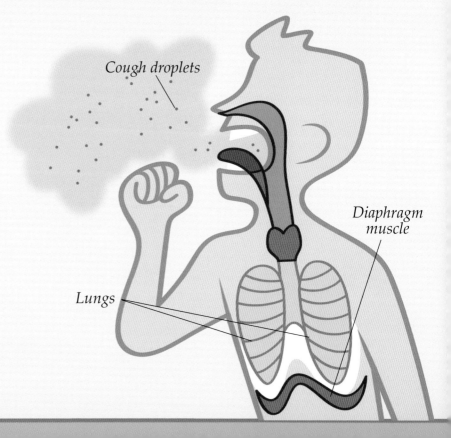

Cough droplets

Diaphragm muscle

Lungs

Down the Back...

A common type of cough is caused by postnasal drip: that is, snot running down from the back of the nose into the throat. The snot irritates the throat and makes it sore. We cough to try to get rid of it.

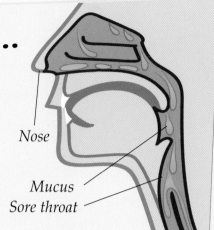

Nose

Mucus
Sore throat

Sometimes, coughs are dry. They don't bring up any mucus or phlegm. Dry coughs happen when our lungs, throat, or airways are irritated by dust or smoke or pollution.

Esophagus

Burning feeling

Stomach

Acid

...Up From Below

A cough can also be caused by digestive difficulties. In some people, after a heavy meal, acid bubbles up from the stomach into the esophagus, causing a burning feeling in the chest. People with this unpleasant condition cough to ease the pain.

Each time we cough, our lungs push out 8 cups (2 L) of air in a jet 6.5 feet (2 m) long. Each cough can contain up to 3,000 droplets of mucus, saliva, and water vapor.

Can You Believe It?

Marine mammals don't breathe through mouths or noses. So they can't cough like we do! Instead, they force air and water out through holes on top of their head, in a tall spout or "blow."

What Are Bronchitis and Pneumonia?

Bronchitis can keep us coughing for weeks or months or years, and that makes muscles in our chest and abdomen tired and strained. Each time we cough, they feel sore.

Bronchitis and pneumonia are long words that tell us we have unpleasant diseases! If left untreated, both can be serious. What's the difference between them? If the airways leading to our lungs (called bronchi) get inflamed or infected and produce too much mucus, doctors say we have bronchitis. If the same thing happens to alveoli, lower down in our lungs, it is called pneumonia. Bronchitis is caused by viruses, industrial dust, air pollution, or smoking. Pneumonia mostly happens when we've been infected by bacteria, a virus, or a fungus, and it causes a high fever and chest pains.

Inflamed airway

Too much mucus

Damaged cilia

There are around 480 million alveoli in each pair of human lungs. If they were all opened up and stretched out on the ground, they would cover a whole tennis court for each lung!

Short of Breath

Sometimes, there is so much mucus filling the airways of people with bronchitis that their bodies cannot get enough oxygen. They breathe in and out very quickly or gasp for breath. They may feel weak and tired or dizzy, and be unable to walk very far.

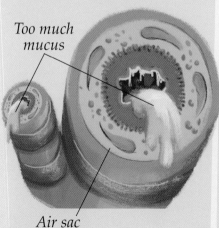

Too much mucus

Air sac (alveolus)

You Sound Sick!

In pneumonia, the alveoli (air sacs in the lungs) fill up with fluid and mucus. So, like people with bronchitis, pneumonia patients can't get enough oxygen.

They feel very sick and struggle to breathe. Doctors diagnose pneumonia by listening for special "crackling" sounds made by fluid inside the alveoli.

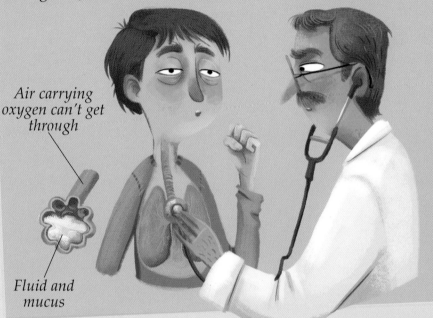

Air carrying oxygen can't get through

Fluid and mucus

Helpful Hint

Don't smoke! In addition to causing cancer and heart problems, smoking is also the cause of four out of five cases of chronic (long-term) bronchitis—and it can give smokers several other nasty lung diseases.

Breathless

Asthma and cystic fibrosis (CF) are two conditions that affect breathing. In asthma, airways swell and become narrow, making it hard for air to get through. In CF, the respiratory system produces mucus that's extremely thick and sticky and often gets infected by bacteria. People living with these conditions sometimes feel as if they are "fighting for breath." This can be frightening and upsetting, but medicines can help asthma patients breathe more easily. For people with CF, antibiotics can fight infections and physical therapy can help keep airways clear.

Wheezing and Gasping

In an asthma attack, the chest often feels tight or full and the breath sounds wheezy. The narrowed airways in the lungs also produce a lot of extra mucus. This makes it very difficult for the lungs to fill with oxygen-rich air. So we gasp and cough.

Air breathed in

Narrow, inflamed, asthmatic airway

Mucus

Fast and Fantastic!

When a person with asthma breathes in the spray from an inhaler, the medicine it contains goes straight to the lungs very quickly. Inhalers help people breathe in two different ways. Preventer inhalers reduce inflammation in the airways; relievers relax the muscles so airways get wider.

Emergency Aid

If an asthma attack is bad or the patient is very old, very young, or very sick, doctors might help them breathe by using a nebulizer machine in the hospital. Nebulizers turn liquid medicine into a mist that is easy for patients to inhale. Sometimes they are given extra oxygen to breathe, too.

Cystic fibrosis is a genetic condition inherited by children from their parents. Symptoms may be mild or severe. Over 30,000 children in the United States are living with CF today.

Disgusting Data

In the past, people took very strange medicines to try to cure asthma, such as raw onion juice mixed with dog hair. These do not work. Do not try this at home!

Shake and Snore

Snoring happens when the muscles in our throat and windpipe relax too much and grow floppy. As our lungs pull air into our body and push it out again, the floppy flesh vibrates (shakes), making a noise.

Quiet, peaceful sleep. Muscles working to keep airway open.

Airway is narrowed but air can get through. Vibration leads to gentle snoring.

Muscles relaxed too much. Airway is blocked. We wake up gasping for air.

No ^Air Way!

For us to breathe properly, the airway leading from our nose to our lungs must be open, so that air flows freely. But sometimes the airway is obstructed, and that's very dangerous! If the airway is blocked by food, drink, or vomit, then we choke. If it's filled with water, we drown. If our muscles are paralyzed, for example, by sickness or an accident, they won't hold the airway open. And if they're relaxed when we sleep—or surrounded by too much fat—then the airway narrows, and we snore. Physical therapy helps to clear airways, and snorers can wear special nasal strips that open the nostrils, allowing more air into the nose.

SNORE!

Being overweight can make you breathless and cause you to snore. Breathlessness is also caused by heart or lung disease or anemia (a shortage of red blood cells).

Surprisingly, yawning is not a sign that we need more air. Some experts think that it is a way of exercising our respiratory system—it stretches lungs, mouth, nose, throat, and windpipe. Others say that yawning helps spread a protective mucus coating inside our lungs.

Cough It Up!

It's happened to most of us—a crumb of food or a sip of water has "gone down the wrong way." Instead of passing along our esophagus into our stomach, it has slipped into our windpipe and blocked it. The best remedy is to cough; that usually clears the obstruction.

Breathing Machine

If we are given an anesthetic (medicine to make us unconscious) so that we don't feel pain during an operation, our breathing becomes weaker. But our airways can be kept open and our lungs filled with air by a machine called a respirator.

Can You Believe It?

The sound made by snoring can be as loud as the noise of a jackhammer—that is, between 50 and 100 decibels. Snoring is loudest when we sleep on our backs.

Feeling anxious? To calm yourself, take two or three deep breaths, then breathe normally. Deep breathing releases natural chemicals in our body that can help improve our mood.

Stay Fit!

Regular exercise makes our hearts stronger and our breathing better. It also increases our alertness, gives us energy, and builds stamina and agility.

Breathe Easy!

Usually, we rely on our bodies to breathe for us, without thinking. But when we get sick, we sometimes find breathing very difficult. If we are really sick, medicines can clear our airways and get rid of infected mucus. But for everyday colds and infections, we can—and we do—rely on the body's own wonderful defenders: snot and phlegm. So how can we help snot and phlegm help us to breathe freely and stay well?

Play a Tune

Singing and playing an instrument (wind or brass) both provide excellent exercise for our respiratory system. They strengthen the muscles in our chest and diaphragm, and increase the amount of air that we breathe in and out of our lungs.

Can You Believe It?

Normally, adults can hold their breath for between 30 and 60 seconds. Any longer is dangerous. DO NOT TRY IT! But free divers train to change the way their bodies use oxygen, and can hold their breath for much longer. The world record is an amazing 22 minutes!

Relax and Go With the Flow

Traditional exercise from Asia, such as yoga and tai chi, use carefully controlled breathing plus slow, gentle movements to improve mental and physical well-being. They are often combined with meditation, which also uses breathing exercises to relax the body and calm and clear the mind.

Ommmmm...

Laugh and have fun! Laughter is lots of quick little breaths, one after the other. It eases stress, reduces anxiety, and makes us feel good.

29

Glossary

Adenoids Lumps of lymph tissue at the back of the nose.

Allergen A substance that causes unpleasant and sometimes dangerous reactions in the body, such as itching or difficulty breathing.

Allergy Condition caused by contact with an allergen.

Alveoli Tiny air-sacs in the lungs. Oxygen passes through the thin walls of alveoli into the blood.

Arteries Blood vessels (tubes) that carry oxygen-rich blood from the heart and lungs to the rest of the body.

Asthma Condition in which airways swell and narrow, causing shortage of breath.

Bacteria Microscopic organisms that live in human bodies and elsewhere. Many are helpful to us; others cause disease.

Bronchitis Condition in which the bronchi (airways leading from the windpipe to the lungs) are inflamed and filled with mucus.

Capillaries Tiny tubes that carry blood from body cells to and from arteries and veins.

Catalyst A substance that helps a chemical reaction work better.

Cilia Microscopic "fingers" in the lining of the respiratory system that help move mucus.

Cystic fibrosis Condition in which people produce mucus that is exceptionally thick, sticky, and likely to get infected.

Diaphragm Layer of muscles at the bottom of the chest, below the lungs.

Esophagus Tube that carries food from the throat to the stomach.

Hay fever Allergic reaction to pollen, causing sneezing, itching, inflammation, and too much mucus.

Histamine Protective chemical produced by body cells. It may cause such symptoms as itching, inflammation, and runny nose when cells come into contact with allergens.

Inflamed Red, painful, and swollen.

Lysozyme Natural bacteria-killing substance in mucus.

Mucus Sticky liquid produced in the respiratory system and other parts of the body. It traps dangerous particles and helps destroy them. It also keeps surfaces inside the body moist and working smoothly.

Oxygen One of the gases in the air we breathe. It is essential for many processes within body cells. Without it, we would die.

Nebulizer Machine that delivers medicine as a fine mist that is easy to breathe.

Phagocytes Special white blood cells that "eat" and destroy bacteria.

Phlegm Thick mucus from the chest, often containing dead white blood cells, bacteria, and saliva.

Pneumonia Condition in which the alveoli in the lungs are inflamed and filled with mucus and fluid.

Reflex Automatic response to a stimulus; activated by a part of our brain we can't control.

Respiratory system Body parts that work together so that we can breathe.

Saliva Watery liquid produced in the mouth. It contains enzymes (natural chemicals) that start to digest our food.

Sinuses Air spaces within the bones of our skull.

Snot Mucus from the nose.

Tonsils Lumps of tissue at the back of the throat.

Toxic Poisonous.

Ulcer Damaged, painful area on the skin or mucus-covered surface inside the body.

Vein Blood vessel (tube) that carries oxygen-poor blood back to the heart and lungs from the rest of the body.

Virus Microorganism that breeds inside the cells of another living creature. Many viruses cause disease.

Index